Night & Day: An Emotional Rollercoaster

Brooke Laing

BookLeaf Publishing

Night & Day: An Emotional Rollercoaster ©
2023 Brooke Laing

All rights reserved.

No part of this publication may be reproduced, stored in a retrieval system, or transmitted, in any form or by any means, electronic, mechanical, photocopying, recording or otherwise, without the prior written permission of the presenters.

Brooke Laing asserts the moral right to be identified as author of this work.

Presentation by *BookLeaf Publishing*

Web: www.bookleafpub.com

E-mail: info@bookleafpub.com

ISBN: 9789357740135

First edition 2023

ACKNOWLEDGEMENT

I'd first of all like to thank my late mum Catherine Bellew for always supporting me when she was alive, my friends & family for taking care of me after that and supporting myself, Taylor and Kieran. A few of my friends who have read a handful of the poems and read drafts or old writings. Lastly to Nicola, for always telling me to do something with them and share them elsewhere, it may be a few years in the making but without you pushing me I'd never have done this, I love you all.

PREFACE

This small collection of poems and writing came to be through a mixture of coping mechanisms for my struggles with mental health and depression, as well as, a way in which to remember lost loved ones or express feelings I couldn't say out loud.

The order in which they appear is the order in which they were written to convey the timeline of my thoughts and feelings over the years. Some are similar in theme so they've been separated.

Waiting

I've been waiting years for this time to come,
You never have time for me. I'd love some.
When we're together, all I do is smile,
Regardless of whether it lasts a while.

I used to care what everyone thought,
Took it to heart and almost lost the plot.
Eventually, I just gave up trying,
I can't even see a point in crying.

Sometimes I just wish that you could see,
How much you really mean to me.
I don't know how to say it to you,
Because I'm scared of what you'd do.

I've lost you once and won't do it again.
But if it comes, I'll deal with it then.
You're my best friend and it's staying that way,
'Cause love's a stupid game to play.

You're gonna have to let yourself see,
That you are always able to come to me,
I won't judge you for anything.
You don't realise it and that's the thing!'

My Best Friend

The first day we met was weird, I'd say,
Still glad you walked into class that day!
From that day on and even now,
You put up with me, so take a bow.

Hoagies, food, all sorts of stuff,
Are the last things we spoke about when we were rough.
A friend for life, now stuck with me,
When I'm old and blind and still can't see.

You're my best friend and I'm happy to say,
That you're the one I know will stay.
You hear me out and understand,
When I fall you help me land.

I'm here for you whenever you need.
You're my favourite little seed.
You've grown on me since we first met,
One thing I can't say about you is 'I regret!'

That's because you're amazing, but most of all,
I hate being with you because I'm so small.
I know you don't like it and that this is cheesy,
That putting up with me aint always easy!

I love you lots, like jelly tots,
There was a lot more but I forgot.
Just wanted to tell you now I'm done
And writing this was rather fun!

The Kiss

Why on earth do I feel like this?
Getting so worked up over one daft kiss!
I feel so bad, but it felt so good.
Spending time with you will always lighten my mood.

I thought all this until tonight,
Your best pal made me feel like shite.
Your smile was like a ray of sun,
But around about now I think I'm done.

I do like you a whole damn lot,
But feeling like this isn't worth a thought.
I should stop, not fall so fast,
But feelings with me come deep and fast.

Feelings come and then they go,
I wish so much that they wouldn't show.
If I had you here right by my side,
My heart and smile would beam with pride.

For just one day, I wish you'd try.
My pride and strength would be so high.
But now I'm done, this is all I'll say.
'I wish it was the same both ways.'

Day One

Today's the day I first met you,
Didn't know what to say or do.
You had my heart from the word 'Hello'
My breath was lost, now breathing slow.

I drop some hints to help you see,
You have no clue what you mean to me.
The butterflies are more than true,
Why can't you see that I love you?

You do not seem to even care,
You make me shiver when you play with my hair.
One more kiss I wish I had.
I'd take you home if we weren't so bad.

The things I'd do to help you see,
Thought: 'You're the one that's meant for me.'
I can't believe how hard I fell,
I even heard some wedding bells.

Another chance I wish you'd ask
This stupid smile is just a mask.
I'm almost done. I can't go on.
When the effort stops, that's it I'm gone.

Some things in life may pass you by,
This love won't budge until we die.
Waking up with you would be my dream,
You and I we're a dream team.

I will like you for the rest of my life,
I saw you as a potential wife.
I can't let you go and you don't know,
My love for you would melt the snow.

Last Words

The same four walls keep closing in,
I might give up and let them win.
It's not so easy to just let go,
I can't tell if you even know!

I thought I was stronger, but not so much.
Feels like I've just lost my touch.
I know it's easier said than done,
But I'll be shining more than the sun.

Goodbyes are never easy to do or say,
When I'm in the sky, I'm there to stay!
And if you ever shed a tear,
I just want you to know that I'll always hear.

Maybe not in person, but always in heart,
I will be around, we'd be never apart.
Now words have never been a strength of mine,
But if you want a hug, then get in line.

Being high but feeling low,
Just hate to let my feelings show.
I know you said just give it time,
I'm sick of hearing the stupid chime.

This hurt will never go away.
I can tell it's here to stay.
I can't go on and let it pass.
So get some vod let's have a glass.

I love you lots, like jelly tots,
And maybe more than a few shots.
So when the time comes to say goodbye,
I'll be leaving this place on a high.

Don't you cry and be all sad,
You're the bestest friends I've ever had.
Stick together and please take care,
You may not see me but I am still there.

Second Best

Forever feeling second best,
A thousand miles below the rest.
I wish that I'd come out on top.
To make these crappy feelings stop.

I do my best to keep you close,
And still can't be the one you chose,
There's always an excuse with you,
Please tell me what more can I do?

Until these stupid feelings ease,
You need to stop being such a tease.
I try my best not to let it show,
But jealousy isn't easy to let go.

One day soon I hope to be,
Back to happy, clumsy old me.
Until you see how much you mean,
My eyes will be forever green.

The Hanging Tree

I think we both should know by now,
The reason why I'm such a cow.
I haven't always been this way,
My moods do change from day to day.

Today it was the final curtain.
I had felt new fear, that was for certain!
My legs went dead, I hit the floor,
I lay there heaped up against the door.

My heart was tight and my eyes were wet,
Keep thinking to myself 'Is it over yet?'.
Just giving up is not too good,
Try to keep going like I know I should.

I know how much I dump on you,
I appreciate all that you really do.
I can't believe that you've stood by,
and listened to my every cry.

I had a scare and almost died.
Those waves were rough, my hair was tied.
One silly thing can't put me down,
I could have jumped, but I'm not a clown.

Stay it out and have some fun,
With you in my life I can never be done.
I want to go and just be free.
And watch you from the hanging tree.

To do that now just would not do.
Why can't I just go see it through?
Whenever I try to leave this place,
I only ever picture your face.

And knowing just how much it hurt,
I can't go and make you feel like dirt.
I can't come out with it another way.
Rhyming is the reason I have to stay.

If I ever let you go,
I just wish for you to know.
That if you ever need to scream,
Just smile and remember me in your day-dream.

Wings

From all the crap that has been spoke,
Mental health is not a joke.
You never know how someone may feel,
When it happens to you, it feels surreal.

You're okay now and doing good,
Whilst I'm stuck here, misunderstood.
If you had known just why I sigh,
You'd sit at night and surely cry.

You think I want to feel this way?
To push all my loved ones further away.
Well, that's messed up and so are you.
These happy pills won't get me through.

I hope that you can understand,
That if you fall then you will land.
You have to fall before you fly.
So, grow some wings and don't say goodbye.

NHS, can I Trust you?

Sitting here, I'm all alone.
The tears are running down my phone.
I'd give my life to kill this pain,
A few more days and I'm insane.

It's been a year, a year too long,
Still no answers. This is just wrong.
It's slowly killing me inside.
It makes me cry and want to hide.

It worries people when I cry.
"No clue what's wrong." Well that's a lie.
I have some words to say to you,
Come back to me when you have a clue.

I'm trying hard just not to break,
This is for depression's sake.
It drains me out and makes me weak,
The pain right now is at its peak.

Can barely even stand to walk,
Can tell I'm hurt just hear me talk.
How can this pain be dismissed?
"Your name is further up the list".

Three months have passed and still no news?
I'm sick of this, you have to choose.
Can't you see how sore I am?
How the hell can I keep calm?

A camera test will do no good.
I'm sick of trying healthy food.
I do it though cause it helps me through,
Come on doctor, I count on you.

There is no point in lying to me.
In a while more I hope to see,
A diagnosis that is true,
NHS, can I trust you?

Alone

I've loved you since the day we met,
From that day on my heart was set.
But nowadays I'm not so sure.
I just don't think that you're mature.

If only you could clearly see,
How much happier you would be with me.
I'd be the one to make you smile,
Just to see it I'd walk a mile.

A thousand more and more each day,
Right by your side I'm here to stay.
I hope that you will always know,
I'll protect you come rain, hail or snow.

Support in all you say and do,
I'm the one who gets you through.
I've realised now and I can see,
You may not be the one for me.

As much as my heart beats for you,
There isn't much more that I could do!
To be with you is all I want,
But all you do is tease and taunt.

From this day on until my last,
I will regret you're in my past.
But from now on you're on your own,
If I can't have you, I'll stay alone.

Head or Heart?

Lying here awake at night,
Thinking about how I make it right?
You have no clue just how I feel,
What I felt today now that was real.

The massive movement in my heart,
It is just so wrong to be apart.
To hurt a friend is oh so wrong,
But without you my days are long.

Do you even feel the same?
I don't think feelings are a game.
If you do, you need to say,
For now, I can only sit and pray.

Pray the choice we make is true,
I be I and you be you.
I'm still not sure just how I feel,
I know she's hurt, but time will heal.

It will take time to sort this out,
But my heart tells me to have no doubt.
You make me laugh and make me smile,
These things I've not done for a while.

To choose between my head and heart,
To think this through, where do I start?
All I know is what I felt.
Just once before did my heart melt.

I never thought I'd feel this way,
Or even that I could be gay.
Never again that I would feel,
So much love, it is surreal.

Relapse

A few months ago, the world shut down,
And in my head I was about to drown.
Before it, all my fight had dropped,
Depression crept in and never stopped.

Being locked inside my broken mind,
The strength to fight I couldn't find.
It got too much for me to take,
So I decided to make the worst mistake.

Of all the things to start again,
Self-harm to try and ease my pain.
How wrong was I to scar for life?
With no one there to take the knife.

So days had passed, then onto weeks,
The colour was draining from my cheeks.
The lack of food and lack of sleep,
It fucked me up and now I'm in too deep.

I try my best to just push through,
Can't be my best when I don't have you.
I know you're here supporting me,
But this shit is dark. I wanna be free.

Free from all this hurt and pain,
To be with you and Nana again.
I know you think I belong down here,
But this pain and shit is too severe.

Each day I stay is hard as fuck,
Cause without you here, days sure do suck.
If I cannot get out of this,
I pray I'm welcomed with a kiss.

To leave this short-lived life behind,
Seems selfish yes, but I'm not blind.
I know the pain that this would cause,
That's just a fraction of what mine 'was'.

I want to stay and beat this game.
Be half the woman you became.
It's just too hard to keep this up.
Like drinking from a broken cup.

Can fill so much then start to break,
Then it's too late and you've made a mistake.
It's pouring now all over the place,
Spilling until it fills its space.

That's what it's like to be like me,
I'm not as strong as you want me to be.
I'm running out of strength and time,
I need some help or I'll start the climb.

I'd like you back

You're on my mind both day and night,
Still in my heart but out of sight.
You held me up and helped me through,
The love I have for you is true.

Our time together was cut too short.
This poem is a last resort.
To let it out and tell you why,
The day we parted made me cry.

We were good together when we were us.
The harder times we did not discuss.
A first love that I will always hold,
I want you back if truth be told.

The only good thing in my life,
I longed for the day you were my wife.
But now its done and we're apart,
There's a constant ache all through my heart.

The ups and downs were good and bad,
The time we spent just made me glad.
To meet someone as great as you,
You are my strength , you are my glue.

To start again and let you know,
To try and let my feelings show.
What would you say to trying again?
Work harder than we did back then.

I had to get my feelings out,
I just don't want to mess about.
Maybe not today or now.
But someday soon if you allow.

I need you back here on my arm.
Your cheeky smile and goofy charm.
You're all I want, it's clear to see,
Why can't you just like me for me?

The good, the bad, the moods and all,
I loved you through it, yet you don't call.
That's all that I am going to say,
But my love for you won't go away.

Heaven

Heaven's just too far away.
I'd love to visit just for one day.
To see you all and see you smile,
Even if it's just for a while.

My place belongs not in the sky,
But down on earth until I die.
Not for some time will I join you,
To leave them now I just can't do.

My time down here is not quite done,
Your smiles were brighter than the sun.
You are my girl, you are my star,
You always said I would go far.

Until the day we meet again,
I will write these poems. I need no pen.
My pixie girl, my heart and soul,
Sarah, now you're gone, there is a hole.

'Not to let it get to me,
Not to let the people see.
To loosen up and go enjoy,
Don't let me down, you're not a toy.'

Those words you shared and tears we cried,
I almost joined you when you died.
You give me strength to keep pushing on,
Until we meet one summer's dawn.

Now I must go and try to sleep.
If I do not, I'll start to weep.
I'm stronger now, more than before,
We shall meet again at heaven's door.

15/08/1960

On this day six decades ago,
Wee Katie Bellew made a show.
Out she came. Her hair dark as night.
A cracking smile, it was some sight.

The youngest of 9 wee bonny wains,
Thank god her maw passed on her brains.
When she grew up she travelled far,
But still had love for a Scottish star.

Bold Les Mckeown had caught her eye,
Front row at concerts, a tartan scarf and tie.
She'd say 'He's mine' constantly to her mother.
But couldn't pull him, so brought home his brother.

She was my mum, my best friend too,
My wee mammy, I really miss you.
Today you'd be out on the piss,
Find some handsome man for a birthday kiss.

Now you're up partying in the sky,
Seems far too long since we said goodbye.
So happy birthday to my best friend,
Party on up there, all my love I send.

'Just Friends'

We are just friends. I tell my heart,
It disagrees and my stomach starts!
There are butterflies going round and round,
And yet again my heart will pound.

I never knew how hard I'd fall,
I suppose that's because I'm rather small.
You took my heart, you took my hand ,
You buried them both deep in the sand.

As long as I know, there's me and you
There's nothing much else I'd rather do.
Than go through life right by your side,
It's sure to be an emotional ride.

Valid

From an early age I'd read about,
The stories of others coming out.
Sometimes, their peers would laugh and shout.
It's actions like these that give me doubt.

Not only because of my own life choice,
But others like me, who have no voice.
Sometimes we're mocked and pushed aside.
How can we say we're filled with Pride?

We're gay, we're bi, we're trans and more!
We're valid too down to our core.
Just let us get on with our lives,
No fights, no anger and god no knives.

We're all the same deep down inside,
Put thoughts, beliefs and opinions aside.
There are bigger problems in this world.
Worse things than hearing abuse being hurled.

Let's come together and end this fight.
Let's spread some joy, some love and light.
Let's all be better versions of ourselves.
Let's put this war back on the shelves.

Capable

From a very young age I've struggled on,
In the belief that happiness was a con.
That was naive of me to think.
As well as coping with a drink.

There are more days than I'd like to admit,
That have ended with some crazy shit.
But as the days just came and went,
Good, bad and ugly wishes sent.

Believe there is no ill intent,
These thoughts took over, I had to vent.
To let pain go and set it free,
To see what happiness can do for me.

I let it in and it was the best choice to make,
It's been so hard with opinions to shake.
It's all okay to go seek help,
Shake yourself, give a slap and skelp.

There is a light at the end of that long tunnel,
As much as this feels like a puzzle.
Keep pushing on and just stay strong,
Your thoughts are never, ever wrong.

Open up during the hardest times,
Even try your hand at rhymes.
Anything that even slightly eases pain,
A long walk in the pouring rain?

I never thought I'd make it here,
Be genuinely happy, healthy, out or queer?
But I am proof that you will get through.
I know that you are capable, too.

Milton Keynes UK
Ingram Content Group UK Ltd.
UKHW020842250823
427479UK00016B/570